Conte...

Above: Loch Tarff, Highland. *Ci-dessus:* Le Loch Tarff, Highland. *Oben:* Loch Tarff im Hochland

Introduction

Beautiful and contrasting countryside runs from the high remote mountains around Glen Affric, across the Great Glen fault line and towards the Moray Firth beaches. Here, Scotland's history is alive. Ancient fortresses like Castle Urquhart bear the scars of conflict down through the centuries. Most famous of all is Culloden, the last battlesite on British soil. There is much evidence of even earlier occupations – standing stones, forts, cairns – silent survivors of past settlements.

Though its roots are in the past, the area is also thoroughly modern – from shopping centres in Inverness to golf at Nairn. Gardens and parks, theatres and visitor centres, ceilidhs and concerts – there is plenty to enjoy in Inverness, Loch Ness and Nairn.

Des montagnes autour de Glen Affric aux plages de Moray Firth, découvrez paysages magnifiques, histoire – château d'Urquhart, site de la bataille de Culloden, menhirs, cairns – et aussi modernisme – centres commerciaux, golf, jardins, parcs, théâtres, « ceilidhs », concerts. La région d'Inverness, du Loch Ness et de Nairn, c'est tout cela.

Eine wunderschöne, kontrastreiche Landschaft erstreckt sich von den Bergen um Glen Affric durch das Great Glen bis zum Moray Firth Strand. Alte Burgen zeugen von einer bewegten Vergangenheit.

Moderne Einkaufszentren, Golf, Gärten, Parks, Theater, Besucherzentren, Ceilidhs und Konzerte machen den Aufenthalt in Inverness, Loch Ness und Nairn zu einem Erlebnis.

1

Inverness: capital of the Highlands

At first sight, the visitor to Inverness might well imagine that the town is of comparatively recent origin – Highland capital it may be, but ancient and venerable architecture is initially hard to find. Its main streets are thronged in summer, its shops bustle and do much business with visitors – there is an almost international flavour as unfamiliar accents are heard buying quality souvenirs, woollens and tweeds, or provisions for the next stage of their Scottish adventure.

But Inverness has always been a meeting place. Here, Highlander and 'Sasunnach' (southerner) met to barter – perhaps at the market originally granted by King William in the twelfth century. In the days when beavers still gnawed birch-bark in the dense forests, their skins would have been exported from the thriving port of Inverness (though they were gone by the sixteenth century). There are records from the twelfth century which indicate that the forests themselves provided Inverness with much timber for shipbuilding.

Yet the clue to the modern appearance of the town lies in its geographical position between the Gaels and the lowlanders. Through the centuries it has suffered at the hands of warring factions. Alexander, Lord of the Isles, the proud

Below: River Ness, Inverness. *Ci-dessous:* La Ness, Inverness. *Unten:* Der Fluo Ness bei Inverness

Top: Inverness Castle and the River Ness. *Above:* St Andrew's Cathedral, Inverness
En haut: Le château d'Inverness et la Ness. *Ci-dessus:* La Cathédrale St Andrew, Inverness
Oben: Burg Inverness und der Fluß Ness. *Oben darunter:* St. Andrew Kathedrale, Inverness

chief of the Clan Donald, burned the town to the ground in 1428, in retaliation for a 'short, sharp shock' treatment from King James I, who had attempted to subdue the Highland clans. Seven times in all, through the Clan Donald's history, it is said, they burned Inverness.

Even after the Union of 1707, when Scotland lost her independence, Inverness was still a target for rebellious factions, though now linked to the south by military roads. Nothing remained of its medieval castles on the strategic site overlooking the Ness – but a seventeenth-century fort, evidence of General Monck's strategy to subdue the Highlands, was rebuilt by General Wade and named Fort George (not to be confused with the later building near Ardersier), as part of the government pro-gramme of garrisoning the troublesome northern parts of the recently united kingdom.

The town was occupied by Jacobite forces briefly in the 1715 uprising. Then, in the '45, the rebel army of Prince Charles Edward Stuart

totally destroyed Wade's fort. Even with the defeat of the rebels the next year, Inverness was still to suffer – the Duke of Cumberland's men pillaged and looted the town in the relentless pursuit of fugitives from Culloden. Thus it comes about that the building that commands the river is the 'modern' Inverness Castle dating from 1834. This red sandstone Victorian edifice is the Sheriff Court and administrative offices.

Yet in spite of history's rough handling, there are some traces to be found of the old town. Though unspectacular in itself, the clock tower on Shore Street, on the east bank of the river, north from the town centre is the only reminder of another fortress. Founded in 1652, 'Oliver's Fort' – from its associations with Oliver Cromwell – was built to hold 1000 men. The English garrison made their mark and may have led to the association that Inverness still has with a pleasing style of speech. In Mackay's

Journey through Scotland, published in 1729, the writer comments on his visit: 'They speak as good English here as at London and with an English accent; and ever since Oliver Cromwell was here they are in their manner and dress entirely English' – all this, with Culloden still seventeen years away!

Non-military traces include late sixteenth-century Abertarff House in Church Street, an example of domestic architecture and once the home of a wealthy burgess. Dunbar's Hospital in Church Street is a century later. Much older is the Clach-na-Cuddain, the stone of the tubs, which carries the town cross and is found in front of the Town House, a nineteenth-century Gothic building, itself, curiously the first place outside London in which a Cabinet Meeting was ever held – Prime Minister Lloyd George's Scottish holiday was interrupted by Irish problems in 1921.

Inverness today is nonetheless an attractive town with a range of amenities from folk clubs to swimming baths, as well as fine walks along the River Ness and through the Ness Islands. Tomnahurich Hill and Craig Phadrig also give fine views and are within easy reach of the town centre.

Left: Kessock Bridge, Inverness. *Below left:* Gardens by the River Ness, Inverness. *Below:* Inverness Museum and Art Gallery

A gauche: « Kessock Bridge », Inverness. *Ci-dessous à gauche:* Jardins au bord de la Ness, Inverness. *Ci-dessous:* Le musée et le musée d'art d'Inverness

Links: Kessock Brücke, Inverness. *Unten links:* Gärten am Fluß Ness, Inverness. *Unten:* Inverness Museum und Kunstgallerie

Around Inverness

The area around Inverness is ideal touring country with sites of scenic and historic interest round almost every corner.

Evidence of ancient civilizations abounds in the form of carved stones, burial cairns and hilltop forts; the remains of the vitrified fort on Craig Phadrig, just west of Inverness, form one of the most notable relics of its kind in Scotland, dating from at least the fifth century BC. It is thought that the stones with which it was constructed became fused together, or 'vitrified' when the surrounding timber was set on fire. There are also several other sites in the area, ringed with barely-discernible ditches or heaps of stones, in some cases with outer rings of standing stones such as the Clava Cairns, just south-east of Culloden, which date from 3000 – 1800 BC.

The Memorial Cairn on Culloden Battlefield (pictured below right) is a Victorian construction. The famous battle is detailed in a later chapter. The Culloden Visitor Centre is a

Left: Old Leanach Cottage, Culloden
A gauche: « Old Leanach Cottage », Culloden
Links: Old Leanach Cottage, Culloden

Left: Beaufort Castle (not open to the public)
A gauche: Le château de Beaufort
Links: Burg Beaufort

fascinating place to visit together with the adjacent thatched Leanach Cottage which is much as it was at the time of the battle and contains a display of domestic relics of the period.

On a much grander scale but less well-preserved is Beauly Priory, at Beauly, thirteen miles west of Inverness. The name Beauly is said to have derived from the French words *beau*

lieu, and this may well be correct because the Frasers of Lovat in whose country Beauly stands were originally Normans, and they were highly conscious of their French blood – even to the extent of using Norman French amongst themselves whenever possible. The seat of the Frasers of Lovat is actually four miles south-west of Beauly at Beaufort Castle, but this is privately owned and not open to the public, unlike Beauly Priory which is a delightful place to visit.

Beauly Priory was founded by John Bisset of Lovat in 1230 but it was allowed to fall into a state of decay after the Reformation and all that remains today is a roofless shell of the church, some of which dates from the thirteenth century and other parts from the fourteenth, fifteenth and sixteenth centuries. The peaceful ruins which remain today provide a stark contrast to the turmoil the area around Inverness has witnessed in the past.

A tour of the area around Inverness will reveal many other equally interesting attractions to visitors, especially those keen on handicrafts. At Beauly, for example, is the Highland Craftpoint Centre, and nearby, at Kirkhill, handfinished soaps are made in an old country church. At Tomatin, a traditional working smithy produces both decorative and functional items, whilst just ten minutes from Inverness on the A862, the Highland Winery at Moniack Castle produces and bottles country wines and liqueurs.

The northern heartlands

This is essential Scotland – farm and glen, moor and hill, forest and loch make touring in this area a visual delight. Foxgloves and willow-herb colour the foreground, birches edge the fir plantations, with glimpses above of bare moor and high summits. South-west of Beauly, Strathglass and the River Beauly lead into the heartland.

The dense woods are threaded by trails in places – at Aigas walks lead out from the field centre. There are several hydro-electric schemes around – but they are mellowed and in scale with the scenery. Visitors familiar with Scotland may be reminded, perhaps, of the flavour of Deeside around Struy, with its river flats, lush green grasses and alders in the water courses. At Cannich, where the valley broadens, there is a choice of Glens Cannich and Affric.

The Cannich road climbs out of the village, giving glimpses into Lower Glen Affric, then twists through birches and under crags. Eventually it opens out in a fine Highland landscape – a cascading burn, bog myrtle and asphodel, glowing heather (in August) and – beyond the dam on Loch Mullardoch, the distant looming westward hills that attract only the fittest of hillwalkers. Plenty of atmosphere and ever-changing patterns as the light picks out browns, greys and the 'tweedy' shades in the pleasing landscape.

Glen Affric offers stunning colours in autumn. The lower glen has oak woodlands and haymaking – as well as a power station at Fasnakyle. Further on there are trails and riverside walks – the Dog Falls are clearly signed from the road. If Strathglass is like Deeside, then parts of Affric echo the Trossachs but on a wilder scale – crags and hummocks, well-clothed in conifers and birch. Unless you are prepared to walk a long, long way west, you must return to Glen Urquhart after your exploration.

There, travelling east towards the Great Glen, the familiar land use pattern returns – farming on the valley bottom, forestry on the slopes, open moorland above. At time of writing, there are extensive forestry felling activities in lower Glen Urquhart, as a reminder that the Highlands of Scotland are not true wilderness – moorlands, hillslopes and water levels reflect the needs of its inhabitants and have been extensively changed over the centuries.

Below: Loch Affric, Glen Affric, Inverness
Ci-dessous: Le Loch Affric, Glen Affric, Inverness
Unten: Loch Affric, Glen Affric, Inverness

Above: Loch Mullardoch from dam, Glenlannich
Ci-dessus: Le Loch Mullardoch vu du barrage, Glenlannich
Oben: Loch Mullardoch von Dam, Glenlannich

Right: Affric Lodge
A droite: « Affric Lodge »
Rechts: Affric Haus

Right: Glen Cannich
A droite: Glen Cannich
Rechts: Glen Cannich

The Battle of Culloden

To portray the Battle of Culloden as the final contest between English and Scots is quite false – there were more Scots on the government side than fought for the rebel clans. Culloden was, instead, the final chapter in a hopeless attempt to restore the old order by winning the British throne for a Catholic Stuart monarch.

The 'tragic hero' in the affair, Charles Edward Stuart, was the grandson of the last Stuart King, James VII of Scotland and II of England, who had fled the country in 1688 in the face of opposition to his support for Catholics. The supporters of the House of Stuart – the 'Jacobites' (from Latin Jacobus, 'James') – had, with continental sympathy and support, fought at Killiecrankie (1689), Sheriffmuir (1715), and Glensheil (1719) in hopeless attempts to restore their line of kings.

In April 1746, the 'Young Pretender' to the throne, with perhaps 5000 men, stood on Culloden Moor in the driving sleet of a late Scottish spring. He had landed at Arisaig on the west coast in the previous July. His campaign had got as far south as Derby, placing all London in great alarm. Government forces had rallied and marched to suppress resistance. But with a string of victories in Scotland, the latest three months before at Falkirk, during his army's retreat northwards, his army now faced 9000 government troops under the Duke of Cumberland.

Nothing was in the Jacobites' favour. The level ground suited manoeuvrable government cavalry and provided a good range for the guns. Tired and ill-fed, the rebels had just failed completely in a night foray to surprise the government forces. Badly advised, with the stinging gale in their faces, out-gunned by heavier artillery, out-numbered by foot and horse, the charge of the Highlanders – when it

was finally unleashed – was ragged and thinned by musketry and grape-shot or held back by persistent and disciplined volleys. Though the right wing did some damage, the left and centre foundered and were driven back. The rout was all over in an hour.

Retribution relentlessly followed. The stories of bravery and heroism of individual Highlanders are counterpointed by the brutalities wreaked upon rebel and innocent local bystander alike. No mercy was shown to the rebel wounded – they were clubbed or bayoneted. The Duke of Cumberland earned on that day his nickname of 'Butcher' – and approved of the brutality as a means of providing a 'final solution' for the rebellious Highlands. Women and children were the victims of atrocities which continued in the area long after the battle – with no distinction made between families who had played no part in the battle and those who were active Jacobite supporters.

Today, the moor is a strange and oppressive place. The National Trust for Scotland are in the process of restoring the immediate landscape to something like its appearance in the eighteenth century. The forestry plantations have already gone; a road which irreverently ran through the Highlanders' graves has been realigned. There are memorial stones which refer to individual clans, as well as other landmarks on the field itself, while the visitor centre is large, tasteful and well-equipped. But, setting rights and wrongs, politics and misplaced hopes aside, the site of the last battle on British soil remains the saddest place in Scotland. The cheery chatter of visitors, the hubbub of tour buses, rattle of crockery and clatter of the gift-shop till make it all the more poignant.

Colour drawing by Jim Proudfoot from Culloden Centre display. Reproduced by kind permission of the National Trust for Scotland
Dessin en couleur de Jim Proudfoot, exposition du « Visitor Centre », Culloden
Farbskizze von Jim Proudfoot vom Culloden Besucherzentrum

Loch Ness and around

Loch Ness has public roads along both banks for most of its length, with perhaps the remotest section in the south-east where the B862 winds into the moors of the Monadliath. Loch Ness is a body of water large enough to have localised weather effects – with mirage conditions in still, warm air not unknown. These are said to be the conditions in which the monster is most likely to be sighted – visitors can draw their own conclusions!

Drumnadrochit stands on the east end of Glen Urquhart, giving access to Strathglass and the beauties of the far west. Also of interest in the glen is the Corriemony Chambered Cairn, a scheduled Ancient Monument excavated in 1952. It is signed from the main road. Within a ring of standing stones is a burial cairn which it is possible to enter, ducking through a passageway to emerge in the centre of the cairn.

But the most famous and popular venue in the area is Urquhart Castle. It stands only minutes from Drumnadrochit where the main road returns to the loch side. Once, with the castles at Inverness above and Invergarry below, it commanded the route through the Great Glen, from the twelfth century onwards. It fell into the hands of Edward I of England in 1296 as part of an early policy of controlling the unruly north, but was retaken by Robert the Bruce in 1308. Too important to remain intact for long in Scotland's troubled history, it saw frequent action, playing a part in the struggle between the Gaelic power base represented by the Lords of the Isles, and the Scottish monarchs.

By the fourteenth century, there were high masonry walls and extensive buildings. In the early sixteenth century, these were ruins. There was a further reconstruction later in the sixteenth century with clan feuds to follow – so that by 1715 it was again uninhabited. Nevertheless it is an impressive site and well worth a visit. To the south, and easily overlooked because of the speed of traffic, is the John Cobb Memorial. He was killed here in 1952 when his attempt on the world water speed record ended with his craft blowing up after hitting a disturbed patch of water. Some suspect that the loch's 'phenomenon' was a possible cause.

Urquhart Castle is one of the reasons for taking the busy west bank road. Visiting places like Dores and Inverfarigaig are good reasons for exploring the east shores. At the first of these, just above Dores, there is a fine end-on view down the loch. Impressive views can also be obtained from the nearby MacBain Memorial

Left: Falls of Foyers. *Above right:* Urquhart Castle. *Right:* Drumnadrochit

A gauche: Les chutes de Foyers. *Ci-dessus à droite:* Château d'Urquhart. *A droite:* « Drumnadrochit »

Links: Wasserfall von Foyers. *Oben rechts:* Burg Urquhart. *Rechts:* Drumnadrochit

Park to the north-east of the village.

Further south, at Inverfarigaig there is an interesting forestry exhibition and forestry walks – turn immediately left, if coming from the north, once across the bridge. (But before you do, look over the east side of the parapet. There is a rapidly-collapsing Wade Bridge of 1732 half-hidden by the trees below you.) One walk from this spot takes you over the burn and upwards steeply, on to Dun Dearduil, an

ancient hill-fort with vitrified stonework, that looms out of the tree-cover.

Continuing southwards, the visitor reaches Foyers with its spectacular falls. This is the site of a hydro-electric development – with water from Loch Mhor, which is higher than Loch Ness to the east, powering the generators. The present scheme is the second – the first started as long ago as 1896 and was the first commercial application of hydro-electricity. It

13

was used in a now-defunct aluminium smelting works.

Glen Moriston on the north-west side of the loch is worth exploring from Invermoriston. Near Ceannacroc Bridge at the west end of the glen is a cairn commemorating Roderick Mackenzie. Of similar build, he drew off pursuit of Prince Charles Edward Stuart when capture seemed likely after his defeat at Culloden. He was shot down and killed by pursuing soldiers, crying 'You have killed your Prince' as he fell. The resultant confusion over identification enabled Charles to make his way from the area and eventually to safety.

Opposite page, top left: Falls of Divach. *Opposite page, top right:* Old Bridge, Invermoriston. *Opposite page, bottom:* Loch Ness, near Dores. *Above:* Loch Ness from the south bank. *Left:* British Legion Piper, Highland Games, Drumnadrochit

Ci-contre, en haut à gauche: Les chutes de Divach. *Ci-contre, en haut à droite:* « Old Bridge », Invermoriston. *Ci-contre, en bas:* Le Loch Ness, près de Dores. *Ci-dessus:* Le Loch Ness, de la rive sud. *A gauche:* Cornemuseur de la Légion Britannique, « Highland Games », Drumnadrochit

Gegenüberliegende Seite, oben links: Wasserfall von Divach. *Gegenüberliegende Seite, oben rechts:* alte Brücke, Invermoriston. *Gegenüberliegende Seite, unten:* Loch Ness, nahe Dores. *Oben:* Loch Ness vom Südufer. *Links:* Pfeifer der Britischen Legion, Hochlandspiele, Drumnadrochit

The Caledonian Canal

It took perhaps a hundred million years for the granite that was formed at present-day Foyers on Loch Ness, and is found today sixty-five miles away at Strontian in Argyll, to drift southwest, along with the rest of the 'top half' of Scotland. The Great Glen is today's evidence of the great wrenching tear which makes such an impressive landscape feature. Loch Ness lies on the fault line, as does Loch Oich and Loch Lochy, making a total of forty-five miles of natural waterway. When the attentions of the authorities turned to the possibility of building a canal, it was clear that along this line would be the best place – with only twenty-two miles of actual constructed canal between the Firth of Lorne and the Moray Firth.

Thomas Telford was asked to survey a route by a London government anxious to stem the tide of emigration and ensure a pool of manpower was kept in the north to fulfil possible military needs in the expanding empire. He came north in 1803, surveyed the route and construction was soon under way. Its highest point was planned at Laggan, over 100 feet above sea level, between Lochs Lochy and Oich. Twenty-nine locks and forty-two gates had to be built.

Nineteen years later, the first ship sailed through the whole length. By 1840, steam tugs were introduced, to aid the passage of sailing vessels. In time, the new generation of larger hulled iron vessels meant the canal had to be reconstructed in 1847.

Today, the canal still operates – a living, working part of industrial heritage that has seen off the challenge of a railway in the Great Glen. A very early example of a purpose-built ship canal, set in outstanding scenery it is still in use by the fishing fleet from Scotland's east coast ports. Yachts and cruisers are part of the Highland scenery, too. There are cruises from Inverness and Fort Augustus, cabin cruisers for hire and the whole system provides superb recreational opportunities.

Below: The Caledonian Canal at Fort Augustus. *Main picture opposite:* The Caledonian Canal at Muirtown Basin, Inverness. *Inset opposite:* The Caledonian Canal at Dochgarroch

Ci-dessous: Le « Caledonian Canal » à Fort Augustus. *Ci-contre:* Le « Caledonian Canal » à « Muirtown Basin », Inverness. *Ci-contre en cartouche:* Le « Caledonian Canal » à Dochgarroch

Unten: Kaledonischer Kanal bei Fort Augustus. *Hauptbild gegenüber:* Kaledonischer Kanal bei Muirtown Basin, Inverness. *Gegenüber, Bildmitte:* Kaledonischer Kanal bei Dochgarroch

Fort Augustus

Fort Augustus must be considered the heart of the Great Glen. Today, it has plenty to interest visitors, especially the bustle of the canal locks in the centre of the village. In the troubled times of the early eighteenth century, when the glens still held clans hostile to the British Government, the settlement, under its former name of Kilchuimein, became an important military garrison. Its first barracks followed the 1715 uprising and soon General Wade had built a large fort, which was captured by the Jacobites during Prince Charles Edward Stuart's campaign. It was replaced by an even larger construction after 1746, the date of the Battle of Culloden.

Johnson and Boswell were well-pleased with the governor of the fort's hospitality after their first day on horseback, on their way down Loch Ness. Boswell's *A Tour of the Hebrides with Dr Johnson* mentions that they found 'all the conveniences of civilised life in the midst of rude mountains' – though this might have been an expression of relief that they did not have to stay at the local 'wretched' inn. (Tourist accommodation has greatly improved in the intervening two hundred years!)

Their course on that day in August 1773 took them down the east bank of Loch Ness, the older of the two present-day roads. Little remains now of the forts that were built at Kilchuimein. After the soldiers left, their equipment shipped out on the brand-new Caledonian Canal, lands and fort were eventually bought by Lord Lovat and donated to the Benedictine Order of Monks. They built the present Abbey and School. There is a nearby museum, near the swing bridge, which tells the whole story of Fort Augustus and surroundings.

Above: Fort Augustus Abbey. *Below:* Fort Augustus
Ci-dessus: L'Abbaye de Fort Augustus. *Ci-dessous:* Fort Augustus
Oben: Fort Augustus Abtei. *Unten:* Fort Augustus

General Wade's roads

Left: General Wade's Bridge at Inverfarigaig

A gauche: « General Wade's Bridge » à Inverfarigaig

Links: General Wade Brücke in Inverfarigaig

Below: The Corrieyairack Pass above Fort Augustus and Loch Ness

Ci-dessous: Le col de Corrieyairack au-dessus de Fort Augustus et du Loch Ness

Unten: Corrieyairack Paß über Fort Augustus und Loch Ness

The two roads that converged on Fort Augustus were the first roads in the Highlands. These are Wade's roads, which General Wade began building in 1726. Between Inverness and Fort Augustus, both the 1726 high road (the B862) and the 1732 shore road (the B852) are open to today's motorists. They traverse wild country that must have seemed even more hostile to the soldiers who laboured through the peat and rock.

The B862 climbing out of Fort Augustus towards Loch Tarff is impressive, with fine views eastwards. At White Bridge, there is a Wade bridge, now bypassed, with the present-day hotel marking the site of a 'Kings-House' – one of a number of inns located on these early roads. The military road that once linked Fort Augustus with Dalwhinnie, on today's main Perth/Inverness route, crosses the high Corrieyairack Pass. Wade may have felt it a challenge to his skills – but the Highland winters won the battle. Used only as a drove road in the early nineteenth century, today the road and its pass at 2500 feet is the haunt of hillwalkers, historians and electricity pylon maintenance crews. The main Great Glen to Speyside route is the A86, further south, surveyed by Telford in 1805.

Loch Ness and the monster

Above: Reconstruction of 'Nessie' at the Loch Ness Monster Exhibition, Drumnadrochit
Ci-dessus: Modèle de « Nessie » au musée du Monstre du Loch Ness, Drumnadrochit
Oben: Darstellung von „Nessie" im Loch Ness Monster Museum, Drumnadrochit

The verdict of 'unproven', peculiar to the Scottish legal system, seems apt to apply to the case of 'The Scientific Establishment versus Nessiteras Rhombopterix'. The pro-monster campaigners are hoping for a successful outcome to a prosecution which they have brought: that a family of unknown animals have a right to inhabit an 800-foot-deep loch in the Scottish Highlands – and that they should be acknowledged as part of Scotland's fauna by zoologists. The establishment and the sceptics claim there is no case to answer – Nessie is a zoological impossibility in the middle of Scotland, no matter how deep the loch, though both parties agree that the publicity over the years has done the local area no harm!

The presentation of the monster as a legal argument is going, perhaps, too far – but that could be said also for some of the explanations put forward by both sides. Over the years Nessie has been identified as a plesiosaurus – a fish-eating, long-extinct reptile, a marine slug, a long necked turtle, a giant seal, a species totally unknown to science, though reported from other lochs in the Scottish Highlands, as well as Canada, Siberia and Africa. She has been hailed as first-cousin to the equally elusive sea-serpent and fringe groups have even tried to tie her up with flying saucers, or other psychic events.

On the other hand, the disbelievers say Nessie is an otter, or many otters in a line, floating vegetation, the wake of a boat, a

Below: Photograph by Mr Lachlan Stuart taken in 1951 (*Daily Express*)
Ci-dessous: Photographie de M. Lachlan Stuart prise en 1951
Unten: Foto von Lachlan Stuart aus dem Jahre 1951

swimming red deer, a cormorant in a mirage, a rock in a mirage, practically anything else that floats in a mirage – or just wish fulfilment.

The number of times the phenomenon appears on film seems to bear a strange inverse relationship to the number of cameras trained on the loch. The high technology of the eighties still has failed to throw a lot of new light – after a flurry of published claims and general excitement in the sixties and seventies.

The Loch Ness and Morar project has proceeded with caution and has at least proved that the Loch could support a number of large aquatic creatures. Their sonar soundings have picked up a number of moving masses at great depth within the loch. Short of some kind of equipment malfunction this kind of record of large aquatic targets has not been satisfactorily explained. Interested visitors should call on the Loch Ness Monster Exhibition at Drum-nadrochit for a very fair assessment of the up-to-date position.

One fact is certain. The spell of the monster is a strong one, causing men to change their careers and alter their whole lives to track it down. Some have even cheated and hoaxed in an effort to gain some strange notoriety – thereby making acceptance by the establishment more difficult. Perhaps we need a monster, as a reassurance that all is not yet rationalised and explained in an increasingly technological and controlled world.

Ever since that fateful day in the thirties when a quiet week on the local paper resulted in a small item about a strange sighting on the loch, the splash caused by the phenomenon's appearance has rippled round the world.

Top: Photograph by R. K. Wilson taken in 1934
Above: Photograph by Mrs Jessie Tait taken in 1969
Below: P. A. MacNab's 1955 photograph
En haut: Photographie de R. K. Wilson prise en 1934
Ci-dessus: Photographie de Mme Jessie Tait prise en 1969
Ci-dessous: Photographie de P. A. MacNab (1955)
Oben: Foto von R. K. Wilson in 1934
Oben darunter: Foto von Frau Jessie Tait aus dem Jahr 1969
Unten: Foto von P. A. MacNab aus dem Jahre 1955

Nairn and around

Nairn, the old county town of Nairnshire, has always had two aspects – one looking to the sea, the other to the land. Even today, the visitor can make out these two towns. Around the harbour area, on the west bank of the river, is the old fishing community. Above the main Elgin-Inverness road is the main shopping area – a different sort of town, once dependent on local agricultural activities. Westwards again, near the sea, lie the mansions and hotels of a seaside resort that benefited from the coming of the railway in the mid-nineteenth century – giving a third facet to Nairn's diverse personality.

Nairn's harbour, now filled with pleasure craft, was built by Thomas Telford in the 1820s. Its herring fishery declined in the 1930s. The fascinating story of the fishing community is told in the Fishertown Museum, where artefacts and photographs bring to life the harshness of the life and the spirit of the community. Further local history information, including relics from Culloden can be found at the Nairn Literary Institute Museum – a charming little museum popular with locals and in every sense the museum of the community.

Other attractions of the town include its golf courses, which have challenged generations of golfers, and its little theatre with a varied programme, found rather unexpectedly in the middle of the fishertown. And, naturally, there are miles of beaches backed by dunes – and lots

Below: Nairn Harbour. *Main picture opposite:* Dulsie Bridge. *Inset opposite:* Nairn Golf Course
Ci-dessous: Le Port de Nairn. *Ci-contre:* « Dulsie Bridge ». *Ci-contre en cartouche:* Terrain de golf de Nairn
Unten: Nairn Hafen. *Hauptbild, gegenüber:* Dulsie Brücke. *mittleres Bild, gegenüber:* Nairn Golfkurs

Above: Fishertown Museum, Nairn. *Ci-dessus:* « Fishertown Museum », Nairn. *Oben:* Fischereimuseum, Nairn

more places to see within a short distance of the town itself.

Between the high moors and the long beaches, there is a great diversity of scenery. This can be seen by visiting Ardclach Bell Tower. Set amid a pleasing pattern of field and forest, this little tower dates from 1655 and was built to call worshippers to its entirely separate church in the valley. In more troubled times it also was an alarm bell rung on the approach of cattle thieves. Tradition has it that the reivers once cut down its bell and threw it in the nearby river, presumably out of exasperation at being continually outwitted, having been spotted from this 'high rock', the translation of Ardclach from the Gaelic.

Further up the valley is the very picturesque Dulsie Bridge, of 1764 – a credit to its military builders. A helpful information board relates how the structure withstood a floodwater height of forty feet above normal in the great Moray floods of 1829.

Just over the border into Moray is the Darnaway Estate Visitor Centre where the visitor can learn about the work of a Scottish estate. At Auldearn on the A96, the National Trust for Scotland look after a seventeenth-century doocot (Scots for dovecot). Also on the little hilltop is an information board giving the plan of the battle of Auldearn fought nearby in 1645. The Marquis of Montrose in support of King Charles, defeated the superior forces of the Covenanters.

Two interesting and contrasting castles in the vicinity are Lochindorb and Brodie. The former lies in ruins on an island in an impressive open setting of seemingly endless moorland. It dates from the thirteenth century. Brodie is a more elegant place in the care of the National Trust for Scotland. It is based on a sixteenth-century Z-plan with later additions. The castle features fine French furniture, English, Continental and Chinese porcelain, and a major painting collection.

Right: Lochindorb Castle.
Below: Brodie Castle. *Bottom left:* Ardclach Church. *Bottom right:* Auldearn Boath Dovecot, near Nairn

A droite: Le château de Lochindorb. *Ci-dessous:* Le château de Brodie. *En bas à gauche:* L'église de Ardclach. *En bas à droite:* « Auldearn Boath Dovecot », près de Nairn

Rechts: Burg Lochindorb. *Unten:* Burg Brodie. *Unten links:* Ardclach Kirche. *Unten rechts:* Auldearn Boath Dovecot bei Nairn

Cawdor Castle

The ancient turreted castle of Cawdor is mellowed and impressive, set beside a rushing river in beautiful gardens with sweeping lawns.

The castle is romantically linked by Shakespeare with Macbeth and dates from the fourteenth century, with the central tower being the most ancient surviving part. Additions and alterations were made during each succeeding century, but principally in the seventeenth century when the gradual conversion of a small defensive fort into a large family mansion was begun.

Lord and Lady Cawdor still occupy it, and their fascinating ancestry includes a gentleman who died of a fit of uncontrollable laughter on hearing of the restoration of Charles II! They share the building and the lovingly kept garden with thousands of visitors in the season.

Inside or out, Cawdor has a delightfully homely atmosphere. It is not a cold monument but a comfortable residence offering a chance to look at Scotland's medieval past. It contains many interesting artefacts including an iron gate taken from Lochindorb Castle in the fifteenth century.

Left: Gardens at Cawdor Castle. *Below left:* The legendary hawthorn tree in Cawdor's dungeon. *Below:* The Drawing Room. *Bottom:* External view

A gauche: Jardins au château de Cawdor. *Ci-dessous à gauche:* Arbre poussant du donjon. *Ci-dessous:* Le salon. *En bas:* Vue extérieure

Links: Gärten von Burg Cawdor. *Unten links:* Ein aus dem Verlies wachsender Baum. *Unten:* Salon. *Unten:* Blick nach Draußen

Above: Floodlit view. *Below left:* Drawbridge at Cawdor. *Below right:* Kitchen at Cawdor

Ci-dessus: Vue illuminée. *Ci-dessous à gauche:* Le Pont-levis à Cawdor. *Ci-dessous à droite:* Cuisine à Cawdor

Oben: angestrahlte Sicht. *Unten links:* Zugbrücke in Cawdor. *Unten rechts:* Küche in Cawdor

Fort George

The connection between Culloden and Fort George is clear – a further solution to a problem that a government in London was fairly sure had been solved with its victory at the battle. However, it was not absolutely certain. The smaller chain of forts in the Great Glen had shown themselves vulnerable in the Jacobite rebellions. As a response, which might be described by the modern term 'overkill', an impregnable fortress was built between 1747 and 1769 on a narrow promontory of land east of Inverness.

It has, in a sense, been garrisoned ever since, long after the possibility of insurrection has passed. Today, in its complete state it is one of the most outstanding fortifications to be seen anywhere in Europe – a 'time-capsule' designed to be self-sufficient, undamaged by attack at any time. Lying only a little distance from the main visitor flow along the Moray and Nairn coast or up the A9 to Inverness, it is sometimes overlooked yet well worth a visit.

To the visitor parking outside the walls, the entrance is impressive enough. Yet this initial impression of the first ravelin – a triangular defensive work beyond the main walls – does not really prepare the visitor for the sheer scale of the work. Only after crossing the principal

Inverness Firth from Fort George
« Inverness Firth » de Fort George
Inverness Förde von Fort George

ditch by a fine wooden bridge, penetrating the walls through the main gate and gaining the high ground of the bastions to right and left, can the full scale of the undertaking be fully appreciated.

The military presence is clear enough from the parade ground and range upon range of buildings below. The curtain-walls and bastions – defensive strongpoints on the walls – make strange symmetrical patterns along the whole length of the fortifications. Light and shadows fall at strange angles on lookout towers and places of arms. Yet only a little study will show each field of possible approach is covered and overlooked by safe places of defence, and each outward plane capable of being swept by fire. The whole effect is quite unexpected. This place of murmuring sea, distant views across

the Firth and the cry of seabirds is really an essay on the deadly art of warfare. Visitors are permitted all round the tops of the defences – take care, as the walls are as broad as a street but unfenced on the inner side, with a drop like a quay-side. Some buildings within the walls, as well as the main visitor centre are also open to visitors.

The architect was William Skinner, fresh from his appointment as 'Military Engineer for North Britain'. His plan, which was little altered during its execution, was for the biggest building project the Highlands had ever seen (not to be exceeded till the Caledonian Canal was built more than fifty years later). John Adam, the eldest son of the famous family of architects, acted as contractor, overseeing all masonwork and brickwork in the fort. The work

went forward on the assumption that an attack could happen at any time. Thus after the eastern walls were completed, activity continued behind a temporary palisade, just in case.

By the time it was ready in 1769, Jacobite activities were becoming unlikely. Social changes throughout the country were going forward – a new Highland economy in place of the clan system was having its effect. Most of the government regiments which were raised from Highland manpower spent some time at Fort George during the course of the eighteenth century. The guns on the rampart were kept in a state of readiness – particularly during the later Napoleonic Wars. Afterwards, though, the structure, beginning to assume dubious military advantage as weaponry improved, was nearly converted into a prison. In 1860 additional seaward armaments were installed – though quickly superseded – and by 1881 army reorganisation required the accommodation once more which the fort could provide. It became the depot of the Seaforth Highlanders, remaining so till 1961. They in turn became the Queen's Own Highlanders by amalgamation with the Cameronians. The Regimental Association and museum is there today, as well as other military presence. In the museum, there is a variety of rather poignant artefacts of war relating to the soldiers of the Queen's Own Highlanders, Seaforth Highlanders and the Queen's Own Cameron Highlanders. The Fort itself is now a scheduled ancient monument.

Left: Views of Fort George
A gauche: Vues de Fort George
Links: Blick von Fort George

Right: Fort George, aerial view. Reproduced by courtesy of Historic Buildings and Monuments
A droite: Fort George, vue aérienne
Rechts: Fort George, Luftblick

Sunset over Loch Ness
Coucher de soleil sur le Loch Ness
Sonnenuntergang über Loch Ness